Seven Steps to Heavenly Chipping

I have been coaching for more than 20 years and spent the last ten of them studying the short game – an area I believe represents the difference between posting a good or disappointing score.

Quite simply, if you have a good short game you can play badly but still score well.

I have found the number one reason for a poor short game is misunderstanding the shot you are about to play. Most golfers have no idea of the simple things: where to land the ball; how much run the shot will have; or what the correct set up is.

Without the correct knowledge of those things and more, the chances of executing a successful shot are small. That's why I am confident this book will help you acquire the short game to improve your score.

However, you **MUST** work through the individual chapters in the correct order, especially the first two as it is essential you understand those two vital aspects of the game before going on to learn the shots themselves.

I hope you enjoy this book and I am sure you will be a much better chipper of the ball after reading and practising the information in it.

Stuart Smith has golf academies at Heydon Grange, Thetford, Old Joes and Feltwell.

In addition to being one of the UK's foremost short game coaches, he has designed the *Putt Easy* and *Connect Easy* training aids which are marketed worldwide by Odyssey and Callaway respectively.

He has also designed a golf club range - Heavenly Hybrid - a full set of hybrid irons which are excellent for senior and female golfers and impossible to shank!

Seven Steps to Heavenly Chipping
Written by: **Stuart Smith**
email: **stuart@stuartsmithgolfacademy.com**
Photography, editing and design
Adrian Milledge
email: **info@golfproactive.com**

Contents

Chapter 1   What is a chip?
Chapter 2   Seven Steps to Heavenly Chipping
Chapter 3   Standard chip
Chapter 4   Running/High Energy chip
Chapter 5   Soft Landing/Low Energy chip
Chapter 6   Lob shot
Chapter 7   Landing zones
Chapter 8   Where most golfers go wrong
Chapter 9   Summary
Chapter 10 Core Board

Chapter One

WHAT IS A CHIP?

A CHIP IS NOT A SHOT THAT GOES UP HIGH AND STOPS IMMEDIATELY.

This, however, is what every golfer thinks - let's get under the ball and help it up.

THIS IS WRONG.

Before you start learning about chipping, let's start with understanding what a chip is. Most golfers misunderstand this shot and visualise it incorrectly, thus reducing the chances of playing it well. A chip shot is one from just off the green, where you need to fly the ball over an obstacle such as:

- Some fairway
- A bunker
- A hump or hollow
- A tier on a green
- A water hazard

So what do you do? You fly the ball for part of the distance and let it roll the rest.

In Figure 1, the shot is executed from a position around the green (position A). It then lands somewhere (position B) and rolls up to the hole (position C).

A chip is a forward flying and forward rolling shot, it is not one that results in the ball stopping dead or spinning backwards. And it doesn't matter if you use a 7-iron or a sand wedge, they are both chips. I like to think of a chip as a shot that is executed less than 20 yards from the green.

A chip can come in various flights, spins and energy/roll and I will work through each of these. Why? Because you may need to stop the ball quickly once it lands.

Or you may be happy to keep the ball low and run it all the way up to the hole.

As you work through the book I will talk about the set up for each variation of chip, how the ball will react for each one and the technique required. I will also explain where you might choose to use these different variations.

Make sure you follow the steps correctly, especially for the set-up. Get the correct set-up for the different chips and you give yourself a great chance of success. In addition, follow the practice drills for each chip and remember to learn your energy/roll values. Without this knowledge your chipping cannot be as successful as it might be.

You will read the word **ENERGY** a lot throughout this book and you must understand this relates to the amount of **ROLL** the chip has. The energy must be controlled on every chip.

A question I always ask my pupils is: 'What is the loft of the club for?' Invariably they say it is to get height. That is **WRONG**. The loft of the club dictates the amount of energy or roll that the ball will have. A 7-iron will have more energy once landed than a sand wedge, this is because the former has less loft than the latter, making the ball roll more. Understand this and you are off to a great start.

Remember **ENERGY EQUALS ROLL**

In each of the different chips you are about to learn, you need to understand the set-up for each shot is a **PRE-SET OF YOUR IMPACT POSITION.**

This means you are starting from the ideal impact position, which you will come back to when striking the ball. This will help reduce unwanted movement and result in more successful chips.

We pre-set this position because you will not have enough time during the stroke to move your core (or chest) into the correct impact position.

So - a chip is a shot that, once landed, will always roll forwards, and you need to allow for this forward energy. The less energy or roll you need on the chip, the harder it is to play

Seven Steps to Heavenly Chipping

Chapter Two

SEVEN STEPS TO HEAVENLY CHIPPING

The Seven Steps to Heavenly Chipping is the routine you should and need to go through for every chip. This way you will give yourself the best possible chance of hitting a successful chip. The seven steps are:

> **ASSESS**
> **VISUALISE YOUR OPTIONS**
> **LANDING ZONE**
> **CLUB/SHOT SELECTION**
> **PRACTISE THE TECHNIQUE**
> **SET UP**
> **STRIKE**

ASSESS

The chip starts as you approach the ball and you should assess:

The lie of the ball
What obstacles are in the way
The condition of the green

The correct diagnosis of the lie is vital in chipping as this will determine what techniques will work best.

- Is the ball in a hole?
- Is it sitting up off the ground?
- Is it a bare lie?
- Is their mud on the ball?
- Is it in the rough, fringe or fairway?

All of the above are the first questions you need to ask yourself and answer. You will struggle to hit a successful chip without knowing these answers. However, most golfers are guilty of ignoring these questions. Instead, they have a quick look at the lie and then hit the chip.

Do you realise, that when your ball is in the rough, it is actually sitting up off the ground 99 per cent of the time? So much so that sometimes the ball is even higher off the ground than it would be when teed up to be hit by your driver.

So, before looking at anything else, check your lie and make sure you know exactly how the ball is lying.

WHAT OBSTACLES ARE IN THEIR WAY?

This seems a simple task as all you have to do is look at the hole from your ball and you can see what's in the way. But what is an obstacle?

Bunkers, mounds, rough grass, bush or tree, path, fairway and fringe are all obstacles.

Everything is an obstacle and what you need to do is identify which ones are major ones to avoid, such as: bunker, bush or tree, path, rough, mound Minor ones, by contrast, are : fairway and fringe. The difference between major and minor obstacles is that you need to avoid the former but can use the latter to help slow your ball down. You need this information before you can start the second step.

CONDITION OF THE GREEN

Why do you need to know this? Simple, in winter the ball will have little roll on a wet or damp green, whereas in the summer it will have lots of roll on a hard dry green. This knowledge or understanding of the green is needed for you to select - the correct landing zone and club/shot. Before any game you should hit a couple of chips onto the putting green and watch what the ball does energy/roll wise as this will really help you later.

VISUALISE YOUR OPTIONS

Visualisation is vital when you are stood next to your ball because it enables you to select the best technique and club for the chip you are about to execute.

You have to

- Visualise the ball landing in potential landing zone areas
- and Visualise it rolling it towards the hole (Figure 2)

Figure 2

You cannot hit successful chips time after time without good preparation. Visualising the shot before playing it is key to great preparation. To develop good visualisation, you have to practise with each of the clubs you want to chip with. You also want to practise the set-up and technique of the styles you are about to learn.

Once you can hit the shots using the different techniques, you will learn how much **ENERGY** the ball has in it. This will enable you to picture the correct chip during a game. Before hitting any chip shot, you should stand behind your ball and visualise it landing on a point - your landing zone then rolling up to the hole. Visualisation will help you to select the correct shot, landing zone and club, giving you the best chance of a good result.

LANDING ZONE

Figure 3

Without calculating the optimum landing zone for every chip you hit, your chances of hitting successful one consistently is low. A landing zone is the area that you require the ball to land on its first bounce before the ball's energy takes it up to the hole (Figure 3)

Hitting a chip without picking a landing zone is like hitting in the dark. When you hit a chip, you might look at the hole, whereas I will look at my landing zone, and focus on hitting the ball hard enough to land there.

Without my landing zone, I cannot chip the ball in or get it close to the hole every time. I would say that this is the least thought about part of a chip. This book will teach you how to pick the correct landing zone every time.

CLUB/SHOT SELECTION

Being able to play various types of chip shot with different clubs will give you many more options when faced with a chip during a game. There is more than one spin to put on a ball when chipping. In the following pages you will learn how to play - the standard chip, running chip, soft landing chip and the lob shot.

Once you have mastered these in practice with different clubs, you will be able to select the correct technique with the best club for the shot you want to play.

Quite often you will be able to choose more than one option and be successful with either. So what will make up your mind to which one is best? That will come down to your knowledge of what techniques work best from which lies or conditions. Most golfers have one chipping style and this limits the chances of successful chipping. The more shot options you have the better your results will be.

PRACTISE YOUR TECHNIQUE

You will learn this in the next chapter. Here, you are trying to practise your impact position with the clubface at the correct angle for the shot selected. You would start by getting yourself into the correct set up position for the chosen technique, as without this, you might not get the correct feeling for the shot you are about to play.

If you were going to hit a lob shot, you would want to practise the clubface coming through impact in an open position.

If your ball is in the rough, you might want to make some practice swings through the rough to get the feeling for what might happen to the club in the real shot. You can then use the information to try and avoid this happening during the shot or to make sure you have chosen the correct shot. This is normally a couple of quick swishes back and through, just to give you the feeling for what is needed during the shot.

SET UP

If you do nothing except get the correct set up every time for a chip, your results will see a massive improvement immediately. Most golfers do not set up correctly for a chip. Why not? It's because a chip is misunderstood. What you think you need to do is wrong, therefore you cannot set up correctly.

The ball at address can be opposite the front foot, in the middle of your stance or even opposite your back foot, but you have to know why it's there, what impact all the different ball positions have on the shot and how you are going to play it.

Figure 4

Figure 5

This book will teach you how to get yourself into a match-winning set up every time for the chip that you have selected. Figure 4 is a good set up, Figure 5 a poor one.

STRIKE

If you manage to get all of the above six parts correct and yet fail to achieve a good strike, you will not execute a good chip. It's that simple.

Once you have gone through the other six parts of chipping, this last one is where you will sink or swim. If you do get the other six wrong, you may still have a chance of hitting a good chip – but you will need some luck for it to end up near the hole.

You are not trying to get the ball up in the air. What you have to do is make the middle of your club strike into the ball in line with the instructions for each technique.

You can rescue a poor set-up with a good, crisp strike, yet 99 per cent of bad chips will be the result of a bad strike. A good strike depends upon how well – and which part of the club – hits the ball.

As you read each chipping style, make sure you recap over the Seven Steps To Heavenly Chipping when practising, as these are needed together with the correct techniques for successful chips.

CHAPTER 3

STANDARD CHIP

We need to begin this section by understanding what each of the chip shots are. So a standard chip is a shot that has the designated amount of energy the club's loft dictates.

We are aiming to strike the ball with the true loft of the club without changing the amount of energy that each club produces to alter the shot. In other words, we are not going to de-loft or open the face at set-up or impact for this chip. The ball will not fly very high nor will it come out low and fast. This chip has a standard flight and roll which is dictated by the club's loft alone. A 7-iron will fly lower and run longer than a pitching wedge.

Once the ball lands on the green, it will simply release towards the hole, without much spin altering the characteristics of the shot. This is the standard chip shot you need in your game. Otherwise you will start worrying when the ball just misses the green and this is bound to lead to a poor shot.

SET UP

Figure 6

Figure 7

- Position the ball just left of centre
- Have your feet close together (no more than 6 inches apart)
- Stand nice and close to the ball (shaft in a more upright position - Figure 7)
- Make sure hands are below your chest

The ball, hands and chest are all in a line and your knees, hips and shoulders should all be square to the target. Your core should favour your left side with 60% of your weight on the left. This will pre-set the perfect impact position for a standard chip. Let's break down each area to make sure you get yourself into this address position and give yourself the best chance of hitting a great chip.

STANCE

Figure 8

- With the ball on the ground, the first step is to make sure you get your feet about six inches apart and positioned correctly in relation to the ball. You are aiming to have the ball just left of centre and your body should be square to the ball to target line.

- You should then position the club behind the ball (Figure 8), ensuring the leading edge is square to the ball to target line. At this point you should not be gripping the club.

- With the grip of the club pointing at your middle and your weight even on both feet, you should lean from the chest over to your left until your chest is over your left heel with 60 per cent of your weight on your left side. Making sure the grip end of the club goes with you, while keeping the leading edge of the club square to the target.

- If you are positioned correctly and the ball is in the correct place in your stance, then the ball your hands and chest should all be in a line.

GRIP

Now you can take your grip. But it is important to take the grip in the correct way.

- Put your left thumb on top of the grip to keep the club in the correct position.

- Then bring your right hand in from the side and place your hand onto the grip (Figure 9).

- Fit your left hand in to feel comfortable with your right without moving it.

At this point you should make sure that your hands are **UNDER** your chest. If you take your grip beforehand, then when you address the ball there is a good chance the club face will open (point to the right - Figure 10) which, in turn, will send all chips to the right. Figure 11 is the correct position.

Figure 9

Figure 10

Figure 11

OVERVIEW

Certain positions will remain the same when chipping and the main one is the relationship between where your hands are in relation to your chest. They need to be directly below your chest and it's essential to keep this position/link for every chip you hit, regardless of where the ball is.

Figure 12

Too many golfers think that they have to have their hands way ahead of the ball, but as you can see, this breaks the relationship between your hands and your chest, giving you inconsistent striking (Figure 12).

Figure 13

Your hands should always be below your chest at address for all chips. Your weight should be slightly favouring your left side, and the ball position for this shot is just left of centre of your stance.

If you take a look at Figure 13 - you can see exactly where the position should be. The ball is left of centre and your hands and chest are in line with the ball.

It must be your chest that moves across, not your waist, as this will keep your head in the correct position. If you allow your waist to be in this position your chest and head will be behind the ball, resulting in a poor chip

This poor set up (Figure 14) is a result of trying to get the ball airborne when chipping and also trying to look at the back of the ball.

At no time when chipping are you trying to get the ball airborne. Remember you do not need height when chipping, just the correct amount of energy once the ball has landed on the green.

Another mistake many golfers make is trying to look at the back of the ball (red dot) when they should be looking at the top of the ball (blue dot) (Figure 15)

If you look at the two different pictures demonstrating set up, you can see which one looks correct, with all parts in the correct place (Figures 13 and 14)

Now you have your body in the correct position in relation to the ball, and the ball is in the correct position in relation to your feet for this chip. Your hands are in the correct position in relation to your chest and the ball.

TECHNIQUE

Figure 16

Figure 17

Regardless of which chip you hit, you must always control the stroke with your shoulders, even though with some of the techniques there is a lot of wrist movement.

The standard chip has only a small amount of wrist movement but it is vital you get right the small amount it does have. Too many golfers have read, been taught or think this is purely a putting stroke. It is not. (The shoulder only movement will give you the soft landing chip - chapter 5).

Yes, the shoulders are dominant in this technique but the wrists are soft and have some movement going back. The key point to remember here is the purpose of the set-up when chipping is to pre-set your **IMPACT** position.

As you can see, the hands are ahead of the club and level with the ball at address, which means your hands MUST pass the ball during the stroke before the club strikes it. Too often I see golfers flicking the club through impact in the hope of getting the ball airborne (Figure 16).

This allows the club to get to the ball first, giving you a poor and inconsistent strike. The other issue is that the chest has moved backwards from its spot, again causing a poor and inconsistent strike.

To teach you the correct feeling for a standard chip, I am going to break your movement down into a couple of moves. The first movement is purely a shoulder movement.

● First of all I want you to make a shoulder only movement so that your hands are level with your right leg. You must also keep your core in its set up position (Figure 17).

Figure 18

- Next you need to make a soft wrist movement, allowing the club to work further back without moving your hands (Figure 18).

Figure 19

- If you take a look at the club face, you will see that the club is now hooded.

Figure 20

- Unlike where it would be for a normal wrist hinge in your golf swing.

Figure 21

The back of my left hand is also facing the ground Ffigure 21).

It is vital you have this soft wrist hinge/movement and not your normal hinge as your normal wrist hinge will open the club too much, leaving you to close it on the way back down into impact.

Figure 22

From here you simply move your shoulders back towards impact, while maintaining the correct wrist set position. This will make sure your hands come through impact first. There is **NO** un-hinging into impact (Figure 22).

Figure 23

The follow through must be restricted and there is **NO** un-hinging even at the point where my left arm and the club almost form a straight line. The trick here is to feel that your left wrist now forms a barrier trying to not let the club head pass it (Figure 23).

With the club face, think about trying to guide it into the back of the ball, instead of getting under or hitting too steeply into it. If you maintain the core position you set at address and you create the correct movement, you will slightly strike down into the ball.

Now you need to practise getting the correct set up and technique before moving to the next stage. You must strike the ball well every time. Without a good consistent strike you will not learn your energy values (roll) for each club.

PRACTICE

The next thing you need to learn is how much energy/roll you get on each club when using this technique. Without this knowledge you cannot pick the correct landing zone. The best way to practise this is to hit the chips from the same position onto a flat green, landing them all in the same place and watching how much energy each club produces. You will notice that the higher the loft of club you use, the less energy the ball will have.

Here are the energy vales for my clubs for a flat chip:

Club	Land (% age)	Roll (% age)
7 iron	20	80
8 iron	25	75
9 iron	33	66
Pitching Wedge	50	50
52 Degree Wedge	60	40
56 Degree Wedge	66	33
60 Degree Wedge	75	25

Knowing how much roll you will get with each club, you can then efficiently practise how to pick the correct landing zones. I would use two or three clubs to begin with, maybe a 7, 9 and sand wedge.

SUMMARY

- A standard chip is where you do not add or de-loft the club at impact
- At address, your ball, hands, chest and weight all favour your left side
- Mainly a shoulder action with a soft wrist hinge in the back swing.

SEVEN STEPS FOR A STANDARD CHIP

1 Assess
This would be the preferred chip, as it is the easiest to play and will give you consistently good results. Your ball will have a nice lie in the fringe or fairway and most of the time you will just have the green to worry about. You can play this chip over an obstacle but in this instance you would have enough green for the ball to land and roll to the hole.

2 Visualise Your Options
After assessing the lie, surroundings and the green, you will now start to visualise the ball landing in different places on the green and rolling up to the hole. What you are trying to do here is to find different possible places where you feel happy to land the ball.

3 Landing Zone
The visualising you have just carried out has given you choices as to where you can land the ball. This step is where you must decide exactly where you plan to land the ball.

4 Club/Shot Selection
After deciding on a landing zone you will be left with a distance of energy/roll the ball requires after landing on the green. Here you must now work out which technique with which club is best. As already mentioned, you have assessed the lie and it is good, therefore the standard chip will probably be best, but not always. You must decide this first and then the club, which will have the correct amount of loft to give the ball its required energy.

5 Practise Technique
Now you are just getting yourself used to the set-up and technique for the shot coming up. It might be worth practising how hard to hit the chip for the ball to land on its landing zone.

6 Set-Up
It is important you get yourself into the correct set up position for the type of chip you are hitting, as having the ball or your core in the wrong position will affect the strike and energy in the shot.

7 Strike
Without question the most important of the Seven Steps To Heavenly Chipping. Without a good crisp strike you will fail to hit a good chip. You are trying to strike into the ball, moving it forwards and not upwards. If you imagine a clock face around the ball, you are trying to guide the middle of your club face into 3 o'clock. Now strike the ball and make sure you hit your landing zone.

Seven Steps to Heavenly Chipping

CHAPTER 4

RUNNING/HIGH ENERGY CHIP

This chip or technique is designed to give the ball a lot more energy than the loft of the club would impart on its own. Using a pitching wedge for this technique will ensure the ball will run as much as it would do if you used a 7-iron and employed the technique for a standard chip (figure 24).

Figure 24

This shot is ideal when you have a lot of green to play with, you have a slope to run up or you want to run the ball through the fringe. In short - anywhere where you want the ball to run on a long way. This technique is also useful when your ball has ended up in a small divot or hole around the green or when you have a tuft behind the ball (Figures 25 & 26).

The flight for this shot will be much lower than any of the other chips. The ball will have lots more energy and roll much further than with any of the other techniques even though you are using the same club.

Figure 25

Figure 26

SET UP

We will again start from the ground upwards. If you look at the address position (Figure 27), you will see that the ball is opposite my right foot The hand position is important for this shot. A lot of golfers misunderstand the correct hand position in relation to the ball

Figure 27

If you look at the address position for this chip (Figure 27), you will see my hands are well forward of the ball but they still have the same position in relation to my chest - underneath it.

Figure 28

From behind (Figure 28) you can see I am square to the target and am very close to the ball.

In addition, my weight favours my left side, which puts my core in the same position as it is for the standard chip.

STANCE

With the ball on the ground, the first step is to make sure you get your feet positioned correctly - about six inches apart. You are aiming to have the ball opposite the middle of your right foot and your body should be square to the ball to target line.

Figure 29

Next, you need to position the club behind the ball, making sure the leading edge is square to the ball to target line. You should **NOT** have taken your grip at this point.

● Place your left thumb onto the top of the grip, which should be below your chest and have your weight even between both feet (Figure 29).

Figure 30

● Lean from the chest over to your left until your chest is favouring your left side, again with 60 per cent of your weight now on your left. Making sure the grip end of the club goes with you (Figure 30).

Most golfers will open the face at this point, but you must make sure you keep the leading edge of the club square to the target. This will help you to deloft the club face - one of the key elements in putting more energy into the chip.

● Now you take your grip.

GRIP

- Bring your right hand in from the side, square on and place it on the grip (Figure 31).

Figure 31

- Add your left hand in to fit with the right, making sure your hands are under your chest.

- If I was to lift the clubhead up and point it out in front of me (Figure 32) with my hands in a neutral position you would be able to see that the clubface is closed.

It should feel as if you are holding onto the side of the grip. If you place your hands on the grip before moving your core across, you will hit all your chips to the right and not get the desired energy.

Figure 32

OVERVIEW

Just as with the standard chip, I have kept the link between my hands and my chest.

Figure 33

Your hands at address must be ahead of the ball, but not ahead of your chest (Figure 33).

Figure 34

- When you have the ball back in your stance it will encourage you to move your core and weight back and this is where most golfers will go wrong (Figure 34).

- This will cause you to hit the chip without the extra energy/roll that this shot needs turning it into a standard chip.

It is vital you keep your hands and chest ahead of the ball at all times in set up and during the stroke.

The set up for this shot is to purposely de-loft the club you are using and to place the ball in a position which will give you a steeper angle of attack into impact. This is how you create the extra energy.

TECHNIQUE

Of all the chips, this one has the most energy. It is vital to achieve the correct movement through impact. You are trying to add energy to the ball.

This will be achieved by de-lofting the clubface setting a steeper angle of attack into impact.

Let's start with the backswing. In the set up, you have gripped the club in a closed position which will help give you the extra energy required. Remember your set up is meant to simply preset your perfect impact position.

The backswing movement is the same as the standard chip. It is only the downswing that changes slightly. As the clubface goes through impact you will need to close the face as this will give you the added energy this shot requires.

● The technique for the back swing is exactly the same as the one you have just learned for the standard chip, so let's go over this movement again. Just as I broke down the movement to give you the correct feeling for a standard chip, I am going to break your movement down into a couple of moves.

Figure 35

Figure 36

● The first movement is purely a shoulder movement. If you take a look at Figure 35, you can see that I have only moved my shoulders until my hands are level with my right leg. That is as far as the hands move.

● Next you need to make a soft wrist movement, allowing the club to work further back without moving your hands (Figure 36). If you take a look at the clubface, you will see the club is now hooded even more than it was for a standard chip.

Figure 37

Figure 38

Many golfers go wrong during this time by trying to open the face – as they do in the swing – so once again it is important to ensure the back of your left hand is also facing the ground. It is vital you have this soft wrist hinge/movement and not your normal hinge as this will open the club too much and leave you to close it on the way back down into impact. The two pictures show the top of the back swing for a standard chip (Figure 37) and a running chip (Figure 38) is a very similar position.

Figure 39

Figure 40

Again, for this technique it is vital you do not let your weight move backwards at any point as this will take the extra run out of the shot and turn it into a standard chip. Looking at the clubface for the two impact positions, you will see that where I have moved my weight backwards I have opened the loft of the club, which ultimately gives the ball less energy.

- Now you are going to make the correct movement back into impact.

- You must start by moving your shoulders back towards the target, driving your hands past the ball.

- Using your wrists, roll the club face over while going through impact. This will help to give you even more energy.

Figure 41

Figure 42

If you take a look at the finish position for a standard chip (Figure 41) and a running chip (Figure 42) you will see the face of the club has remained square for the standard chip but has closed for the running chip. There is very little follow-through for this technique, as the club will be striking down into the back of the ball and there is a good chance it will dig into the ground.

PRACTICE

Once you have the required technique, you need to practise a few things such as:

- How much extra roll you get with this technique

- How to chip out of divots/holes around the green

- Practise chipping out of rough or areas with a tuft of grass behind the ball

- Practise running the ball up hills and through the fringe

With this shot and knowledge you can turn an awkward chip into a relatively easy one.

SUMMARY

- A running chip is a high energy shot that will stay low to the ground and roll a long way

- The ball must be back in your stance while your hands and core are still left of centre

- Take your grip after positioning your core and club in their correct place

- The backswing is the same technique as the standard chip

- Do not allow your weight to move backwards at any point during the stroke

- Roll your hands over as you strike the ball.

- This chip shot is ideal when you have ended in a small hole around the green or in thicker grass.

- Watch out for moving backwards during the stroke.

SEVEN STEPS FOR A RUNNING CHIP

1 ASSESS

When looking, you might assess the situation and decide the best way to get the ball close to the hole is to play the chip with high energy, giving the ball extra roll. You would not have a bunker to go over but you could have a mound, some rough, fairway or fringe to deal with. There is a good chance the lie is bad and you are not able to play any of the other techniques without risk.

2 VISUALISE YOUR OPTIONS

After assessing the lie, surroundings and the green, you will now start to visualise the ball landing in different places on and off the green and rolling up to the hole. If you have a good lie with no real hazards in the way, you are simply trying to find different possible places where you feel happy to land the ball. If it is a bad lie you will have to work out how the ball will react out of the lie and where you can land the ball. Sometimes you can use a mound, some rough, fairway or fringe to help slow the ball down.

3 LANDING ZONE

The visualising you have just carried out has given you choices for where you can land the ball. This step is where you must decide exactly where you plan to land it.

4 CLUB/SHOT SELECTION

After deciding on a landing zone you will be left with a distance of energy/roll that the ball requires to take it up to the hole after pitching. Here you must now work out which technique together with which club is best. As already mentioned, you have assessed the lie and surroundings and a running chip is best. You must decide this first and then the club, which will have the correct amount of loft to give the ball its required energy.

5 PRACTISE TECHNIQUE

Now you are just getting yourself used to the set up and technique for the shot coming up. It might be worth practising how hard to hit the chip so the ball pitches on its landing zone. Make sure you practise closing the face at impact as this will help with the extra roll required; and practise from a similar lie if it is a bad one. This will help prepare you for what will happen to the club when playing the shot.

6 SET UP

It is important you get yourself into the correct set up position for the type of chip you are hitting - having the ball or your core in the wrong position will affect the strike and energy in the shot. The ball is back in your stance but your core and hands are left of centre.

7 STRIKE

Without question the most important of the Seven Steps To Heavenly Chipping. You will fail to hit a good chip without a good crisp strike. You are trying to strike into the ball, moving it forwards and not upwards. If you imagine a clock face around the ball, you are trying to guide the middle of your clubface into 3 o'clock. Make sure you commit to the strike as this technique really needs commitment. Now strike the ball and ensure you hit your landing zone.

CHAPTER 5

SOFT LANDING CHIP

What is a soft landing chip?

- It has a soft flight
- Lands softly on the green
- Has a gentle low energy release towards the hole

When you have been told to make a putting stroke for your chip, this is the shot you are executing. This shot would normally be used when you have a very fast downhill chip and you need to carry the fringe or you have very little green between the edge of the green and the hole.

You need to have a good lie for this technique in short grass or have a ball that is sitting up in slightly longer grass. This is the **ONLY** chip where you use the putting stroke technique -there is **NO** wrist movement here.

SET UP

Figure 43

Figure 44

From the ground upwards, you will see (Figure 43) that he ball is just inside my left heel and I am standing very close to it (Figure 44). This will make the heel of the club sit off the ground; this, in turn, will encourage a strike nearer the toe of the club. This helps to deaden the strike, reducing energy. My core is again favouring my left side, with 60 per cent of my weight also on my left, and my hands are below my chest.

Having the ball slightly ahead of my core will help encourage a weaker strike as it is much harder to hit down into impact. This will allow me to hit the shot with very low energy as once again I am pre-setting my impact position.

STANCE

To get into the correct set up, start by

Standing up to the ball with the ball opposite your left heel, and your feet only a few inches apart (Figure 45).

Figure 45

- Using your right hand to hold the club, place the club behind the ball and move the shaft into an upright position so that the heel of the club is off the ground.

- You should still be holding the club just with your right hand (Figure 45) and the shaft should be pointing at your middle. At this point, moving from your chest, you should lean on to your left side.

Figure 46

The temptation here is to place too much weight behind the ball, which will move your core backwards and give you an inconsistent strike (Figure 46).

Even though you want to hit the shot with very little power, your core must be left of centre as this will give you the correct impact position for a consistent strike. The technique that you use for this shot will enable you to hit the ball with little energy.

GRIP

You can take your normal grip, as you do not need to influence the club face for this shot. The hands should be under your chest. If you take a look at look arms in this set up (Figure 47) and compare it to any of the other set styles, you will see that my arms are slightly more bent – just as if I was about to putt. You can choose to use your putting grip for this chip but I prefer to use my normal grip for all chips.

Figure 47

OVERVIEW

Again the link between your chest and hands has remained intact. With the ball slightly further forwards in your stance, you will certainly reduce the ball's energy when playing the shot.

The problem here is you may tend to lean back to try to help the ball up but this technique is simply to help the ball on its way when you are faced with a fast or downhill chip. You may also need to make sure you are nice and close to the ball as you are only using your shoulders for this shot. Set up needs to feel almost as if you are about to putt.

TECHNIQUE

This is the only chipping stroke that is the same as the putting stroke, (Figures 48 and 49) as you do not use any wrists for this shot. The temptation here is for you to flick your wrists through impact as in a bid to help the ball up (Figure 50) - something you are certainly not trying to do.

Figure 48

Figure 49

Figure 50

Figure 51

- You need to rock the shoulders back and through at a nice even pace

- Your hands should be level with the ball as the club strikes it (Figure 51)

I would control the power by the length of the stroke back and through, rather than speed. Speeding up will give you too much energy when landing. Again it is vital you keep your core on its address position. This shot is easy to mis-strike as there is hardly any power in it. The judgement of the strike has to be more accurate than with other chips as there are no wrists. You are relying purely on correct timing with your shoulders.

Figure 52 Figure 53

To achieve the correct feeling for this technique I would like you to take your set up, place the grip end of the club into your belly button, and hold the club down the shaft.

Simply rock your shoulders back and through, just as if you were putting. At no point should the grip come away from your body, as this will change the shot and probably give you a poor strike (Figure 52 and 53).

Once you have practised that for a while, you can try it on the grass. Hold the club as normal and try the same movement with your shoulders, making sure that you do not allow any wrist movement back or through. You are aiming to brush the grass every time as you go through the impact area. If you do not touch the grass, you will catch the ball too high up and it will roll too far. If the club digs in, you will either duff the ball or you will have too much energy in it.

PRACTICE

I recommend practising this stroke in some nice fluffy fringe first to help you attain the correct strike and to build confidence. Once you have more confidence, I would then start to use this technique on different clubs so that you can see how much or how little energy each club can have when using this technique. When practising, you need to learn how much or how little roll each club will give you, as this shot will only be used in a few places. Remember this technique requires the best timing.

SUMMARY

- At address ensure you stand close to the ball and the toe of your club is in the ground
- The ball should be opposite your forward foot at address
- This is purely a shoulder movement, just like a putt. No wrist action is needed
- This shot is to be played when you have a nice lie and you need a delicate chip
- Be careful not to use your wrists

SEVEN STEPS FOR A SOFT LANDING CHIP

1 ASSESS

When looking, you might assess the situation and decide the best way to get the ball close to the hole is to play the chip with low energy. This could be because you have an obstacle in the way, the pin is cut close to the fringe leaving little green to work with or it is a fast downhill chip.

2 VISUALISE YOUR OPTIONS

After assessing the lie, surroundings and the green, you will now start to visualise the ball landing in different places on the green and rolling up to the hole. You would normally decide to land the ball on the green as this is the best surface and one that will give you a more consistent reaction.

3 LANDING ZONE

The visualising you have just carried out has given you choices for where you can land the ball. This step is to decide exactly where you plan to land it.

4 CLUB/SHOT SELECTION

After choosing a landing zone you will be left with a distance of energy/roll the ball needs after pitching to take it to the hole. Now you must work out which technique and with which club is best. The lower the club's loft you use, the easier it will be to get a good strike.

5 PRACTISE TECHNIQUE

Now you are just getting yourself used to the set up and technique for the shot coming up, It might be worth practising how hard to hit the chip for the ball to land on its landing zone. You should practise moving your shoulders back and through with the amount of power you think you will need for the chip to come.

6 SET UP

It is key you get yourself into the correct set up position for the type of chip you are hitting - having the ball or your core positioned wrongly will affect the shot's strike and energy.

7 STRIKE

Without question this the most important step of the Seven Steps To Heavenly Chipping - without a good crisp strike you will fail to hit a good chip. You're trying to strike into the ball, moving it forwards and not upwards.
If you imagine a clock face around the ball, you are trying to guide the middle of your club face into 3 o'clock. Do NOT help the ball up, simply make sure you get a good strike and let both the club and the technique do their jobs. Now strike the ball and make sure you hit your landing zone.

CHAPTER 6

LOB SHOT

I would like to see this shot renamed the 'stop quickly shot' or 'very low energy shot' as, rather than thinking you need to lob it up high, this is what you need it to do. Because it is called the lob shot, most golfers try to get the ball up high, which then makes the chance of failure much greater. You would normally play this shot when you are behind an obstacle, such as a bunker or a mound, and the pin is close to the edge of the green leaving you very little space in which to land the ball and stop it near the hole. A lob shot requires very low energy once landed on a green. The best way to create very low energy is to play the shot with as much loft as possible on the club. As a result, it's odds on the ball will go up high.

SET UP

Figure 54

What you are trying to achieve here is a set up that means when you return to this position at impact, you will hit the ball that has very low energy once it lands on the green. If you do not get the correct set up for this extremely hard shot, the chances are you will play a poor one. If you take a look at the address position in Figure 54, you can see the ball is well forward in my narrow stance, and my chest is slightly left of centre with my hands below it. From behind (Figure 55) you can see that my toes, knees, hips and shoulders are all square to each other, but pointing left (open) of the target. The clubface is square to the target, but open (pointing to the right) to my alignment. My hands are low down so that they are closer to the ground, and I am standing further away for this chip than for all the others.

Figure 55

Figure 56

Too many golfers have the ball too far back in their stance for this chip (Figure 56) which will make the angle of attack into the ball too steep.

STANCE

Figure 57

Figure 58

- Position the club behind the ball making sure it is square to the target (Figure 57 and 58)

Figure 59

Figure 60

- Lean the club backwards while keeping the leading edge square to the target (Figure 59 and 60). It is too easy here to twist the club open to the target line and this must not happen.

- The shaft will now be pointing to the right of you. What you must do now, is to ignore the clubhead, but at the same time keep it at the set angle and stand square to the shaft.

- Now you can place your feet six inches apart

- Your core will be in the same position as for all the other chips, with 60 per cent of your weight on your left and your hands below your chest

Figure 61

Figure 62

The ball position will appear to be in two different ones in relation to your feet due to your open alignment. If you look at this set up standing square to the ball to target line, the ball is forward in my stance (Figure 61). But if you change angle so that it is square to my alignment line, the ball now appears to be more central (Figure 62).

GRIP

Figure 63

You must take your normal grip while the club is in this position and you will notice you are holding onto the side of the grip. In setting your stance correct, you have already altered the angle. If you lift the club up you will see the clubface is open - pointing right (Figure 63). This is a much better and safer way to achieve the correct grip, as opposed to simply twisting the clubface open and then taking your grip. That way can lead to the SHANKS.

OVERVIEW

This set up is very similar to that of a bunker shot in which you are trying to increase the loft of the club in an attempt to lower the energy in the ball once landed.

Getting the set up correct for a shot like this will make the difference between a good strike with the required low energy and a bad shot. I see too many golfers have the ball back in their stance for this type of shot, which makes the angle of attack steeper and means you have to be more accurate with your strike.

The only time it is okay to have the ball back is when your ball is in longer grass or a tuft is behind it and a steeper angle of attack is needed.

TECHNIQUE

The idea of the lob shot is to play a shot, which once landed on the green, has very low energy. The more lofted or open the clubface at impact, the less energy you will produce. The set up has just given you a great start in having an open clubface at impact. What you must do during your swing is maintain this open face throughout. Too many golfers will start from a good position but will then close the face during the swing, giving the ball more energy.

Figure 64

Figure 65

As you can see from Figure 64, my wrists are active and play a pivotal role in this technique. But just like all the other chips it is still my shoulders that control the movement. The trick here is to make a stroke, which slides the clubface between the ball and the ground at exactly the time the club overtakes your hands (Figure 65).

Figure 66

After impact, you need to keep the clubface open (Figure 70) and not let it close.

First of all, I want you to practise the correct movement through impact. Without this movement, you will fail to execute this shot correctly.

Once you have achieved the correct set up, I want you to waggle the club back and through, just by using your wrists (Figures 67 and 68). Your hands should not really move from side to side for this exercise. You must make sure the clubface remains open on the way back, open at impact and open in the follow through.

Figure 67

As you can see, I have used a loft indicator to show you how open I am keeping the face of my club at all times. If I was to make my normal release going through impact (Figure 69), you would see the loft of the club dramatically closing.

It is during the follow through where you will find this movement the trickiest - a good check is to make sure the back of your left hand is pointing up to the sky in an unnatural position (Figure 68).

Figure 68

Figure 69

35

Secondly, you need to add your shoulders and full wrist hinge into the movement.

Figure 70

Turn your shoulders so that your hands are level with your right leg (same initial movement as the standard chip) (Figure 70).

Figure 71

Make an open hinge quickly, just like the one you have been practising – making sure you keep the clubface open (Figure 71).

Figure 72

Now you need to turn your shoulders back towards the target making sure that your hands lead and that you don't whip the clubhead in too early (Figure 72).

Figure 73

At the last moment just before impact you whip the club though with your wrists, allowing the clubhead to keep moving throughout. This time to a higher position and all the time keeping the face open throughout the release (Figure 73).

PRACTICE

Once you have the hang of this technique, I would practise this shot from different lies and distances. I would also practise swinging longer, shorter, slower and faster to see what happens to the ball. Please remember that if you need to use this shot in a game, it means you are in a tricky position. You need to have confidence in playing this shot, which only practice will give you. I prefer to keep the stroke shorter while whipping it through quicker, which gives a more consistent strike.

SUMMARY

- Set up is vital – your feet, knees, hips and shoulders are square with one another but they are all open to the target
- Keep your club face square to the target at address
- Even though this is a lob shot your core must still be favouring your left hand side, with 60 per cent of your weight also on your left
- Make sure you keep the clubface open at all times
- This shot is played when you are behind an obstacle and need the ball to stop quickly
- Watch out you do not flick your wrists to early

SEVEN STEPS FOR A LOB SHOT

1 ASSESS

When looking, you might assess the situation and decide the best way to get the ball close to the hole is to play the chip with very low energy. This could be because you have an obstacle in the way and you will have a decent lie.

2 VISUALISE YOUR OPTIONS

After assessing the lie, surroundings and the green, you will now start to visualise the ball landing in different places on the green and rolling up to the hole. You would normally decide it is best to pitch the ball on the green as this is the best surface to land it on because it gives you a more consistent reaction. You must visualise the landing and rolling part of this shot, not the ball going up high, as it's the landing that's important. The height is purely a result of using a lofted club, which will give you the low energy.

3 LANDING ZONE

The visualising you have just carried out has shown you where to land the ball. You will not have too many options for this shot and little room for error.

4 CLUB/SHOT SELECTION

After deciding on a landing zone, you will be left with a distance of energy/roll that the ball requires after landing on the green. Here you must now work out which technique together with which club is best. As it is the lob shot you will need your most lofted.

5 PRACTISE TECHNIQUE

Now you are just getting yourself used to the set up and technique for the shot coming up, it might be worth practising how hard to hit the chip for the ball to land on its landing zone. Make sure you practise in the grass where the ball is lying - the longer the grass the more it will try and twist your club closed.

6 SET UP

It is important you get yourself into the correct set up position for the type of chip you are hitting, as having the ball or your core in the wrong position will affect the strike and energy in the shot. Remember to lean the shaft back and not twist the face open.

7 STRIKE

Without question the most important of the Seven Steps To Heavenly Chipping - without a good crisp strike you will fail to hit a good chip. This chip is different: as you are trying to get the grooves on your club to spin the bottom of the ball, the strike has to be perfect. Strike the ball and make sure you hit your landing zone.

Seven Steps to Heavenly Chipping

CHAPTER 7

LANDING ZONES

A landing zone or area is the spot you need the ball to land on its first bounce. This will be mostly on the green but will sometimes be off the green. Without first picking a correct landing zone, you will find it difficult to hit successful chips. Picking the landing zone means that you have already worked out the required amount of energy your shot needs.

Figure 74

When you watch the Tour professionals eye up a chip, you will sometimes see them walk to the side (Figure 74). They do this because they are looking for a landing zone while at the same time trying to work out how much energy the ball needs to take it up to the hole from the landing zone (Figure 75).

The previous chapters have shown you the various set up and techniques for the different chips. What I will now teach you is how to practise landing the ball in the correct place and the energy values for each shot.

Picking a landing zone is one thing, being able to land the ball there is another. Therefore you will need to practise landing the ball in the correct place.

If you take a look at this picture (Figure 76), you can see I have placed six clubs on the ground.

These are all about one yard apart and can be placed anywhere, not necessarily on a green and, starting with your most lofted club, practise with five balls and try to land them in between each shaft, using the standard chip first of all.

If you miss one, I suggest you start again until you can get all five in a row. Starting again is good practice – in a game you will get only one chance. Once you have completed five with your first club, move down to the next lofted club and so on, until you have managed to land all of the clubs you wish to chip with in each of the zones.

I would then start again with the most lofted club using a different technique. The different energy values on the ball will alter how hard you need to hit it in order for you to land within each zone. This is something that you should practise regularly as most golfers are unable to hit the correct landing zone often enough in a game.

Figure 75

Figure 76

Once you are comfortable and proficient at landing the ball in the correct place, I would move on to a green.

This time start again with your most lofted club and practice landing the ball in the same place each time (Figure 77). This time, however, alter the techniques so that you can see how differently the ball reacts upon landing.

All you have to do is learn how much roll you get with the same club using different techniques. This knowledge will help you to decide which shot is best when playing. Again, go through this routine for all clubs and see your expertise improve.

Figure 77

Figure 78

A great way to test your ability now is to play a game I call 'round the clock' (Figure 78). This is where you place eight balls in the fringe around a green and, with your most lofted, chip the ball as close to the hole as possible each time. It is up to you where you land the ball and which technique you use for each shot. This will get you up to speed on which shot works best from where, which is what you need to know in a game situation. If you hit a poor shot, **TOUGH**. Do not take it again as this takes away the genuine feel of playing in a real game. Once you have had a go with all clubs, I would place the balls further away from the green and start again.

SUMMARY

- Your landing zone is the area you would like your ball to have its first bounce
- Practise landing the ball between different shafts
- Practise landing the ball in the same spot on the green with the different techniques to learn your energy values
- Play the 'round the clock' game to build up your ability to pick the best shot from different positions around the green.

CHAPTER 8

WHERE MOST GOLFERS GO WRONG

This chapter aims to demonstrate where I believe most golfers go wrong when chipping. If, after trying out each of the chipping techniques, you are still having trouble hitting consistently accurate shots, this section will help you to see where you might be going wrong. Most golfers try to apply all they have read, watched and learnt into their chipping, without fully understanding any of it.

- The shot most golfers see when chipping is wrong
- The ball position most golfers use to play the shot they see is wrong
- The technique is wrong

So let's start with the

STANCE

The two most common faults I see are:

- The ball is too far back in your stance
- Your core is too far back

BALL POSITION

Make sure that you are fully aware of which chipping technique you are practising or playing and then think about the ball position. Remember, for more energy/roll have the ball further back in your stance; for less energy/roll have the ball further forward.

CORE

The main reason golfers have their core too far back is because they think they need to get under the ball. All you have to remember about your core position is, that regardless of which chip shot you are playing, your chest should be favouring your left side, likewise 60 per cent of your weight. Once you have taken the correct stance, remember to lean from the chest (Figure 79) **NOT** your hips over to your left every time (Figure 80). This will guarantee a much better core position at the start of every chip.

Figure 79

Figure 80

GRIP

The only problem I see with your grip, is that you will establish it before positioning the clubface, feet and core first. Certainly for the running chip and the lob shot you must make sure to set up your grip last.

TECHNIQUE

- Moving your core backwards during the stroke
- Flicking your wrists

As you can see from Figure 81 my weight has moved backwards, and I have flicked my wrists going through impact – the two swing faults I see all the time.

Let's start by understanding why these two poor movements happen. It is very simple, yet again it is the thought of trying to get under the ball and help it up is the main cause. The other reason for moving your weight backwards is – in a full golf swing your weight should move backwards in the back swing and then transfer through as you strike the ball. Making the process of keeping your weight on your left side in the back swing, unnatural.

Figure 81

CORE

When you are in the correct address position for any of the chips, you should feel more pressure in your left foot. What you need to practice is to keep that pressure there, the whole time throughout the shot. If you keep the pressure there, then you will not move your core back and have a great chance of a good strike.

FLICK

This is also very common. This is because golfers try to get the ball airborne when they should be focusing on striking the ball forwards. Remember the loft of the club dictates energy/roll and not height, so there is no need to flick under the ball.

The key area to think about here is to make sure that your hands pass the ball before the club head strikes it. Even though on the lob shot, you are not trying to get height, you are always trying to strike the ball forwards and allowing the loft of the club to control the energy.

CHAPTER 9

SUMMARY

STANDARD CHIP

- A standard chip is where you do not add or de-loft the club at impact

- At address, your ball, hands, chest and weight all favour your left side

- Mainly a shoulder action with a soft wrist hinge in the back swing.

- Learn your energy values for the clubs you wish to chip with

- This chip would normally be played when you are just off the green with no obstacles to go over

- Be careful not to move your weight back or flick your wrists.

SEVEN STEPS FOR A STANDARD CHIP

1 ASSESS

This would be the preferred chip as it is the easiest to play and will give you consistently good results. Your ball will have a nice lie in the fringe or fairway and most of the time you will just have the green to worry about. You can play this chip over an obstacle but, in this instance, you would have enough green for the ball to land and roll to the hole.

2 VISUALISE YOUR OPTIONS

After assessing the lie, surroundings and the green, you will now start to visualise the ball landing in different places on the green and rolling up to the hole. What you are trying to do here is to find different possible places where you feel happy to land the ball.

3 LANDING ZONE

The visualising you have just carried out has given you choices for where you can land the ball. This step is where you must decide exactly where you plan to land the ball.

4 CLUB/SHOT SELECTION

After deciding on a landing zone you will be left with a distance of energy/roll the ball needs after landing on the green. Here you must now work out which technique and club is best. As already mentioned, you have assessed the lie and it is good, therefore the standard chip will probably be best but not always. You must decide this first and then which club has the correct amount of loft to give the ball its required energy.

5 PRACTISE TECHNIQUE

Now you are just getting yourself used to the set up and technique for the shot coming up, it might be worth practising how hard to hit the chip for the ball to pitch on its landing zone.

6 SET UP

It is important you get yourself into the correct set up position for the type of chip you are hitting, as having the ball or your core in the wrong position will affect the strike and energy in the shot.

7 STRIKE

Without question the most important of the Seven Steps To Heavenly Chipping, without a good crisp strike you will fail to hit a good chip. You're trying to strike into the ball, moving it forwards and not upwards. If you imagine a clock face around the ball, you are trying to guide the middle of your club face into 3 o'clock. Now strike the ball and make sure you hit your landing zone.

RUNNING CHIP

- A running chip is a high energy shot that will stay low to the ground and roll a long way
- The ball must be back in your stance while your hands and core are still left of centre
- Take your grip after positioning your core in its correct place
- The backswing is the same technique as the standard chip
- Do not allow your weight to move backwards at any point during the stroke
- As you strike the ball, roll your hands over
- This chip shot is ideal when you have ended in a small hole around the green or in thicker grass.
- Watch out for moving backwards during the stroke.

SEVEN STEPS FOR A RUNING CHIP

1 ASSESS

When looking, you might assess the situation and decide the best way to get close to the hole is to play the chip with high energy to give the ball extra roll. You would not have a bunker to go over but you could have a mound, some rough, fairway or fringe to deal with. There is a good chance the lie is bad and you are not able to play any of the other techniques without risk.

2 VISUALISE YOUR OPTIONS

After assessing the lie, surroundings and the green, you will now start to visualise the ball landing in different places on the green and rolling up to the hole. If you have a good lie with no real hazards in the way, you are simply trying to find different possible places where you feel happy to land the ball. If it is a bad lie you will have to work out how the ball will react out of the lie and where you can land it. Sometimes you can use a mound, some rough, fairway or fringe to help slow the ball down.

3 LANDING ZONE

The visualising you have just carried out has given you choices for where you can land the ball. This step is where you must decide exactly where you plan to land the ball.

4 CLUB/SHOT SELECTION

After deciding upon a landing zone you will be left with a distance of energy/roll the ball requires after landing on the green. Here you must now work out which technique and club is best. As already mentioned, you have assessed the lie and surroundings and a running chip is best. You must decide this first and then the club, which will have the correct amount of loft to give the ball its required energy.

5 PRACTISE TECHNIQUE

Now you are just getting yourself used to the set up and technique for the shot coming up. It might be worth practicing how hard to hit the chip for the ball to land on its landing zone. Make sure you practice closing the face at impact, as this will help with the extra roll required, and to practice from a similar lie if it is a bad one. This will help prepare you for what will happen to the club when playing the shot.

6 SET UP

It is important you get yourself into the correct set up position for the type of chip you are hitting, as having the ball or your core in the wrong position will affect the strike and energy in the shot.

7 STRIKE

Without question the most important of the Seven Steps To Heavenly Chipping. Without a good crisp strike you will fail to hit a good chip. You're trying to strike into the ball, moving it forwards and not upwards. If you imagine a clock face around the ball, you are trying to guide the middle of your club face into 3 o'clock. Make sure you commit to the strike as this technique really needs commitment. Now strike the ball and make sure you hit your landing zone.

SOFT LANDING CHIP

- At address make sure you stand nice and close to the ball and the toe of your club is in the ground

- The ball should be opposite your forward foot at address

- This is purely a shoulder movement, just like a putt. No wrist action is needed

- This shot is to be played when you have a nice lie and you need a delicate chip

- Be careful not to use your wrists.

SEVEN STEPS FOR A SOFT LANDING CHIP

1 ASSESS

When looking, you might assess the situation and decide the best way to get the ball close to the hole is to play the chip with low energy. This could be because you have an obstacle in the way, the pin is cut close to the fringe leaving little green to work with or it is a fast downhill chip.

2 VISUALISE YOUR OPTIONS

After assessing the lie, surroundings and the green, you will now start to visualise the ball landing in different places on the green and rolling up to the hole. You would normally decide it is best to pitch the ball on the green as this is the best surface to land a ball on as it gives you a more consistent reaction.

3 LANDING ZONE

The visualising you have just carried out has given you choices as to where you can land the ball. This step is where you must decide exactly where you plan to land it.

4 CLUB/SHOT SELECTION

After deciding on a landing zone you will be left with a distance of energy/roll the ball requires after landing on the green. Here you must now work out which technique and club is best. The lower the loft of the club you can use, the easier the shot will be to strike!

5 PRACTISE TECHNIQUE

Now you are just getting yourself used to the set up and technique for the shot coming up it might be worth practising how hard to hit the chip for the ball to land on its landing zone. You should practise moving your shoulders back and through with the amount of power you think you will need for the chip to come.

6 SET UP

It is important you get yourself into the correct set up position for the type of chip you are hitting, as having the ball or your core in the wrong position will affect the strike and energy in the shot.

7 STRIKE

Without question the most important of the Seven Steps To Heavenly Chipping. Without a good crisp strike you will fail to hit a good chip. You're trying to strike into the ball, moving it forwards and not upwards. If you imagine a clock face around the ball, you are trying to guide the middle of your club face into 3 o'clock. DO NOT help the ball up, simply make sure you get a good strike and let both the club and the technique do their job. Now strike the ball and make sure you hit your landing zone.

LOB SHOT

- Set up is vital – your feet, knees, hips and shoulders are square with one another but they are all open to the target

- Keep your club face square to the target at address

- Even though this is a lob shot your core must still be left of centre; 60 per cent of your weight must also be on your left

- Make sure you keep the clubface open at all times

- This shot is played when you are behind an obstacle and need the ball to stop quickly

- Watch out you do not flick your wrists too early

SEVEN STEPS FOR A LOB SHOT

1 ASSESS

When looking, you might assess the situation and decide the best way to get the ball close to the hole is to play the chip with very low energy. This could be because you have an obstacle in the way and you will have a decent lie.

2 VISUALISE YOUR OPTIONS

After assessing the lie, surroundings and the green, you will now start to visualize the ball landing in different places on the green and rolling up to the hole. You would normally decide that it is best to pitch the ball on the green, as this is the best surface to land a ball on because it will give you a more consistent reaction. You must visualise the landing and rolling part of this shot, not the ball going up high as it's the landing that is important. The height is purely a result of using a lofted club which will give you the low energy.

3 LANDING ZONE

The visualising you have just carried out has shown you where to land the ball. You will not have too many options for this shot and little room for error.

4 CLUB SHOT/SELECTION

After deciding upon a landing zone you will be left with a distance of energy/roll the ball requires after landing on the green. Here you must now work out which technique and club are best. As it is the lob shot you will need your most lofted club.

5 PRACTISE TECHNIQUE

Now you are just getting yourself used to the set up and technique for the shot coming up, it might be worth practising how hard to hit the chip for the ball to pitch on its landing zone. Make sure you practice in the grass where the ball is lying - the longer the grass the more it will try and twist your club closed.

6 SET UP

It is important you get yourself into the correct set up position for the type of chip you are hitting, as having the ball or your core in the wrong position will affect the strike and energy in the shot.

7 STRIKE

Without question the most important of the Seven Steps To Heavenly Chipping - without a good crisp strike you will fail to hit a good chip. This chip is different as you are trying to get the grooves on your club to spin the bottom of the ball - the strike has to be perfect. Strike the ball and make sure you hit your landing zone.

Seven Steps to Heavenly Chipping

CHAPTER 10

CORE BOARD

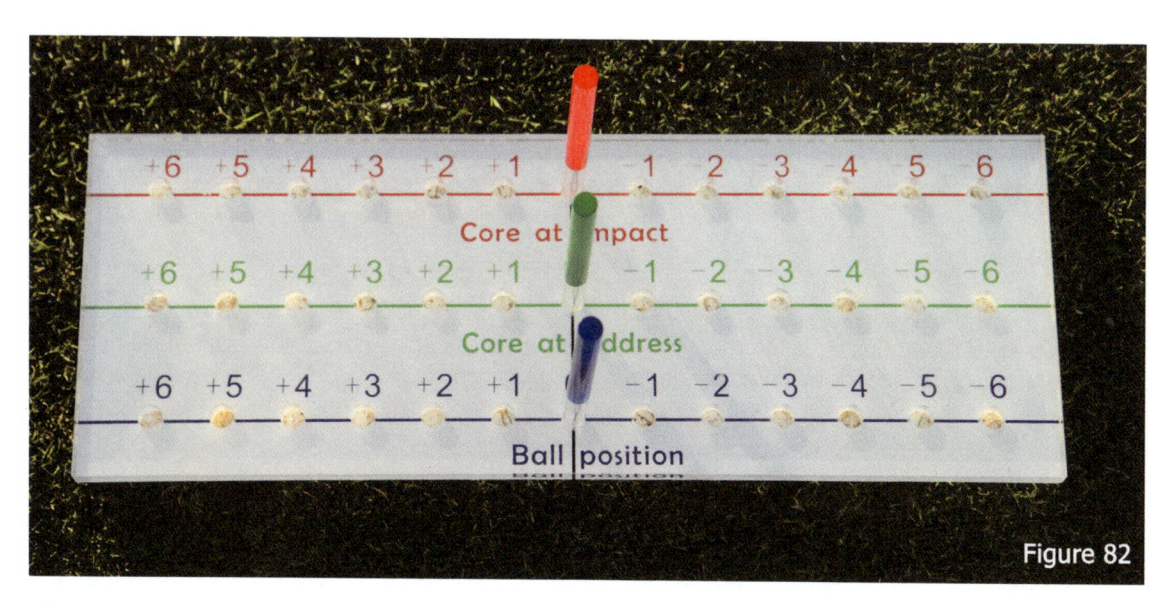

Figure 82

The Core Board (Figure 82) is a practice aid I have designed to help golfers understand the correct ball, set up and impact positions plus the link between all three.

I designed this specifically because I found my pupils were unable to grasp the exact start position and impact position for all golf shots – especially in the short game. The Core Board helps golfers to understand easily the correct positioning both at address and impact.

Using the board when practising will help you achieve the correct positions. Its purpose is to create the correct link between the ball position and your core (core will relate to your chest at all times). Most golfers break this connection most of the time, yet keeping this correct link will give you accurate and consistent shots. Accompanying this book with a Core Board will help you to become a much better chipper sooner.

How the Core Board works

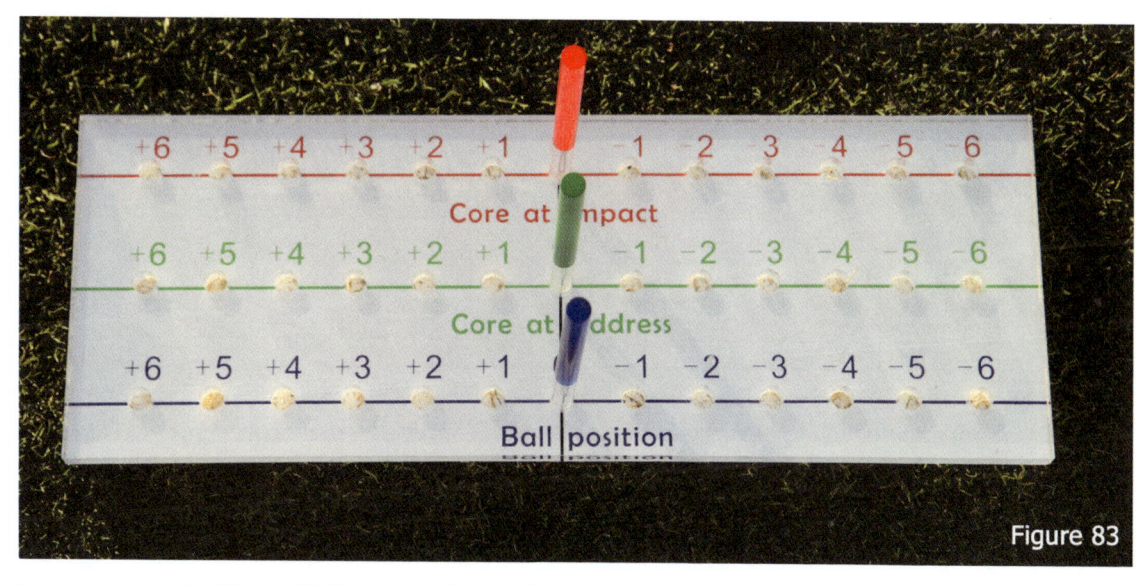

Figure 83

As you can see in Figure 83 there are three coloured rows with pegs and a black centre line. Correct positioning of this black line is vital for you to understand, learn and improve while using this board. This line must always be in the centre of your heels.

Figure 84

If the line is not equidistant between your heels (Figures 84 and 85) the numbers will not make the differences you need to learn. The board also needs to be between your feet and the ball, making sure your toes (Figure 86) are nearer to the board than the ball, otherwise your shaft may hit the pegs (Figure 87). If you take a look at the board, you can see that the black line is 0 and the other lines go from +6 to -6.

Figure 86

Figure 87

The three coloured rows are:

BLUE ROW
Ball Position: The idea of this peg is to teach you the correct ball position for each of the different shots in golf. Ball position is relevant to two things: the mid-point of your stance (between your feet) and where it is in relation to your core (chest). It is possible to have the ball in the wrong position in relation to your feet and still hit a successful shot – as long as the ball is in a good position in relation to your core. Correct ball positioning along with correct core positioning is vital in improving both your accuracy and consistency.

GREEN ROW
Core at Address: The purpose of this peg is to get your body and hands in the perfect address position. This will give you the best chance of getting into the required impact position and improve your chances of making a great shot. The idea is to position your chest (core) over the green peg, with your hands directly under your chest. This is where you want to be at impact in order to enable you to execute a successful chip.

Really, all you are trying to do at address is to PRE SET your IMPACT POSITION. This will enable low body and weight movement, which is vital when chipping, and in turn brings consistency and accuracy. As my core moves to be over the green peg, my weight will also move. If you look at the left image (Figure 88) you can see my core is +2 on the core board and my weight is favouring my left side. In the other image (Figure 89) my core is -2 and my weight is now on my right side.

Your core position at address and impact WILL dictate where your weight is, and this means your core positioning at address is vital. The link and correct positioning (ball, body, hands) between the Blue and Green pegs will give you the best chance of achieving the correct impact position.

Figure 88

Figure 89

RED ROW
Core at Impact: This is the one where everything comes together - IMPACT! Get this aspect of your impact position correct and your chances of playing a great shot are now much greater than the chances of playing a bad one. It really is that easy.

Once you get going, most of you will achieve the blue and green peg positions but it is this red peg that will let you down. Why? The answer is most golfers believe a chip is a shot that goes up. You move your core backwards during the stroke (Figure 90) (as you are trying to get under the ball) and this means you will be in the wrong position at impact.

You have not left your core or returned it to the correct impact position, and the result is normally a thin across the other side of the green or a duffed shot where the ball moves about two yards. For every successful chip you hit, without exception, you will have the correct ball position (blue peg) linked with the correct core position (red peg) (Figure 91). In very simple terms: get your core in the red position for all the different chips and your chipping will improve beyond belief.

Figure 90

Figure 91

Let's re-cap. The idea of the board is to teach you the correct ball position in relation to the centre of your stance and your core, then to get you set up correctly, giving you the best possible chance of getting into the perfect impact position time after time.

SUMMARY

The Core Board will help you to:

- Achieve a great set up for every shot
- Show you exactly where you should be at impact
- Teach you how to hit different chips

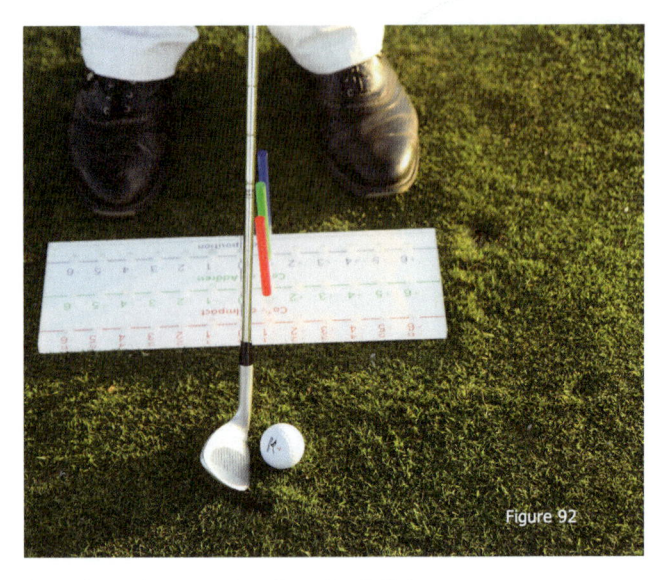

Figure 92

Core board set up for Standard Chip

Figure 93

Core board set up for Running Chip

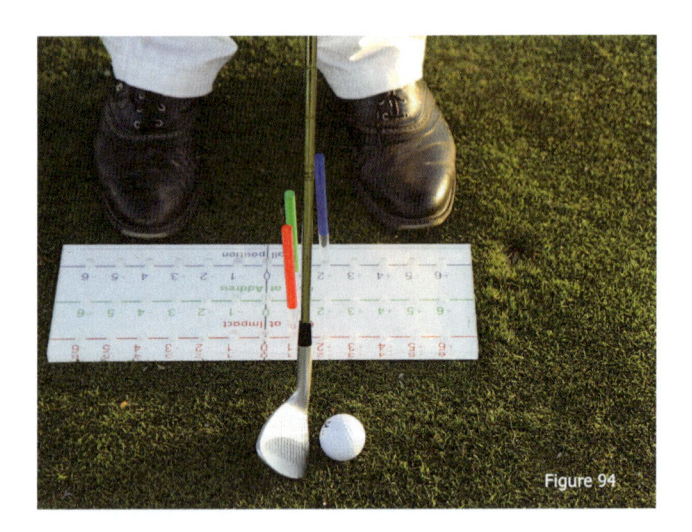

Figure 94

Core board set up for Soft Landing Chip

Figure 95

Core board set up for Lob shot

To purchase a Core Board please visit
www.stuartsmithgolfacademy.com

Hopefully this book has changed how you view chipping and, with
working through it, I am confident in you becoming a better chipper of the ball.

Good chipping is all about having options when faced with a chip.
It is a great feeling to stand over a chip and know that you can use any
one of three clubs and any one of two techniques to chip your ball in.

Good luck

golfpluscruise.com
ULTIMATE GOLF & CRUISE HOLIDAYS

2015 MASTERS
AT AUGUSTA NATIONAL

3NTS US MASTERS AND 7NT 5* CARIBBEAN CRUISE

Includes a free night in Fort Lauderdale
8th - 19th April 2015

This great offer starts from only £5499 & combines watching the 2015 US Masters and enjoying a fabulous 7 night cruise on the 5 star Celebrity Silhouette.

Availability is limited so to avoid disappointment call

FREEPHONE
0800 0736 549

and talk to our specialist reservation staff

www.golfpluscruise.com

ABTA L5791 | ATOL 10531 | CRUISENATION

For your financial protection all bookings are with Cruise Nation, a registered member of ABTA L5791. Cruise Nation also operates under ATOL 10531. For further information see our Terms & Conditions.

Find us on Facebook | Follow us on twitter

Golf Plus Cruise Limited, Company Reg No: 08488257

Made in the USA
Charleston, SC
16 December 2014